STORYTELLER:
JEWISH STORIES

First published in this edition in 2011 by
Evans Brothers Limited
2a Portman Mansions
Chiltern Street
London W1U 6NR

British Library Cataloguing Data
  Ganeri, Anita
  Jewish stories. - (Storyteller)
  1.Judaism - Juvenile literature
  I.Title II.Phillips, Rachel
  296
  ISBN 9780237544157

Editor: Victoria Brooker
Series Editor: Su Swallow
Designer: Simon Borrough
Illustrations: Rachael Phillips, Allied Artists
Production: Jenny Mulvanny
Consultant: Jonathan Gorsky, educational advisor at the Council for Christians and Jews, London

Acknowledgements
The author and publishers would like to thank the following for permission to reproduce copyright material: **page 6** Trip/E James **page 9** Mark le Poer Trench/Performing Arts Library **page 11 and back cover** Trip/P Mitchell **page 19 and back cover** Trip/I Genut **page 20** (left) Trip/H Rogers (right) Zefa **page 25** Trip/S Shapiro **page 26** Trip/R Seale **page 27 and back cover** Trip/H Rogers **page 28** Trip/A Tovy
A Shofar and a Coffee Cauldron adapted by permission of the MIRIAM ALTSHULER LITERARY AGENCY on behalf of Yaffa Eliach. Copyright ©1982 by Yaffa Eliach.

STORYTELLER: JEWISH STORIES

Anita Ganeri

Illustrations by Rachael Phillips

Evans Brothers Limited

Introduction

Jewish Stories

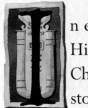
In each of the world's six main faiths Hinduism, Judaism, Buddhism, Christianity, Islam and Sikhism - stories play a very important part. They have been used for many hundreds of years to teach people about their faith in a way which makes difficult messages easier to understand. Many stories tell of times in the lives of religious teachers, leaders, gods and goddesses. Others explain mysterious events such as how the world was created or what happens when we die. Many have a strong moral or lesson to teach.

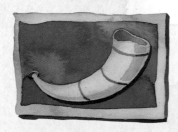

The stories in this book come from the Jewish faith. According to Jewish scriptures, the first Jew was Abraham, a man who lived in the Middle East more about 4,000 years ago. He taught his family and everyone he met to worship one God, instead of many different gods. Jews believe that God made a covenant (an agreement) with Abraham. God said that the Jews should live wise and just lives. Then he would look after them for ever.

In their daily lives and at festival times, Jews listen to stories to help them remember their long history. You can read some of these stories in this book.

Contents

The Story of Creation

In the beginning, God created Heaven and Earth. But the Earth was dark and had no features, or shape or living things.

"Let there be light," God said, and suddenly the Earth was filled with light. Then God separated the light from the darkness. He called the light day, and the darkness night. This was the first day of creation.

On the second day, God created the sky and set it high above the Earth. On the third day, he made the seas and the dry land. God said, "Let grass sprout up from the ground, and plants bearing seeds so that new plants can grow, and fruit trees of every kind." Soon the Earth was covered with grass, plants and trees with their branches filled with fruit. God was pleased with what he saw.

When the fourth day dawned, God said, "Let lights appear in the sky, to divide day from night. They will be signs to show the passing of the seasons, the days and the years, and will shine light on the Earth." So God placed two great lights in the sky - the Sun to rule the day and the Moon to rule the night.

Did you know?

In September or October, Jews celebrate God's creation of the world at the festival of Rosh Hashanah. This is the start of the New Year. It is also the time when Jews think about the wrong things they have done in the past year and promise to put things right. On the eve of Rosh Hashanah, people share pieces of apple dipped in honey to wish each other a sweet new year.

Did you know?

Each week, Jewish people keep the seventh day holy for rest and worship. They call it Shabbat. It begins at sunset on Friday, when two candles are lit to welcome Shabbat in. Then a prayer is said, called the kiddush, before the family sits down to enjoy a meal together. On Saturday morning, many Jews go to the synagogue. Shabbat ends when the first stars appear on Saturday night.

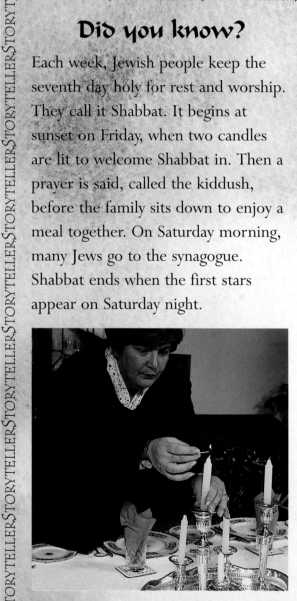

On the fifth day, God ordered the seas to fill with fish, and flocks of birds flew and sang in the air. Then God created the great whales and all the living things that crawl and run about the Earth. And God blessed them all.

On the sixth day, God created all the creatures that live on Earth, cattle, wild beasts and creeping things. Then he made a man and a woman in his own image and likeness. He blessed them and said, "You will rule over the Earth, and over every living thing on Earth, the birds, the fish and the great whales. Your children will rule after you. See the green plants and trees filled with fruit. They will be your food, and food for all living things that move and breathe." God looked at everything he had created and he saw that it was good. Now the work of creation was finished and the Earth was filled with life. On the seventh day, God rested from all his work. He blessed the seventh day and declared it holy for ever, a day on which no work should be done. And this is the story of creation.

Joseph and his Brothers

Long ago, Jacob lived in the land of Canaan with his twelve strong sons. The second youngest was Joseph, who was seventeen years old. Because Joseph was born in Jacob's old age, Jacob loved him best of all. He gave Joseph a present, a beautiful coat of many colours. Joseph's brothers were furious. They hated Joseph because he was their father's favourite and had not a good word to say about him. To make matters worse, Joseph told them about two dreams he had had in which he saw his whole family bowing down to honour him. This time, even his loving father scolded him for showing off.

One day, Joseph's brothers went off to feed their flocks of sheep, and Jacob sent Joseph after them.

"Go and see how they are getting on," he said. "Then come back and tell me the news."

But when the brothers saw Joseph coming, they hatched a plot to get rid of him once and for all. They stripped off his fine coat and flung him into a pit. Later they sold him to some passing merchants for twenty pieces of silver. Then they killed a goat and smeared Joseph's coat with its blood. "We'll tell our father that a wild beast has eaten him," they agreed.

When Jacob saw the blood-stained coat, he was heart-broken. He wept and wept, and no one could comfort him. ▶

Did you know?

The coat which Jacob gives to Joseph is often described as a coat of many colours. But no one is sure what it was really like. It might have been woven with coloured threads, or been decorated with embroidery, or even had long, flowing sleeves. It was certainly a special present and showed that Joseph was Jacob's favourite son. This is what had made Joseph's brothers so jealous.

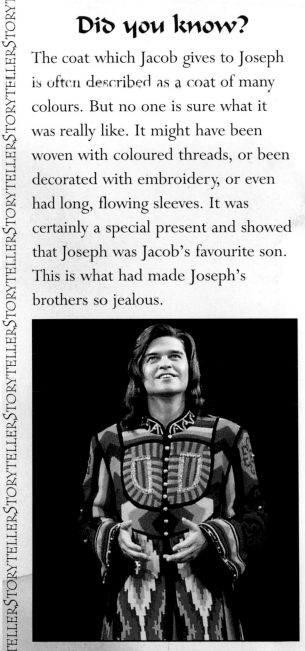

The merchants were bound for Egypt. There they sold Joseph to Potiphar, one of Pharaoh's chief officers. Joseph quickly became Potiphar's most trusted servant and was put in charge of his house. But Potiphar's wife told lies about Joseph and had him thrown into prison. There he became famous for interpreting the dreams of the other prisoners. Among them was Pharaoh's butler. Joseph told the butler that he would soon be released from prison and go back to his job in the royal palace. And this is exactly what happened. The grateful butler promised never to forget Joseph's kindness and to help Joseph if ever he could.

Several years passed. One night, Pharaoh himself had a strange dream. He dreamt he was standing by the banks of the River Nile when he saw seven fine, fat cows come out of the water, followed by seven thin, bony cows. The thin, bony cows ate the fat ones up. Next he dreamt that seven fine, ripe stalks of corn were swallowed up by seven shrivelled, unhealthy stalks. When he woke up, Pharaoh was deeply puzzled. He sent for the wisest men in the land but none could tell him what his dreams meant.

"Call for the prisoner, Joseph, Your Majesty," his butler said, remembering his promise. "He will help you, I'm sure."

So the Pharaoh sent for Joseph and told him his dreams.

"Your Majesty," said Joseph. "Both of your dreams mean the same thing. For God is showing you what he is going to do. Egypt will have seven years of plenty, with rich harvests of grain. But seven years of famine will follow. Your Majesty should appoint a wise man to be governor of Egypt. Give him the job of storing crops from the years of plenty to share out during the famine. Then no one in Egypt need go hungry."

The Pharaoh was so pleased with this advice that he gave the job to Joseph. He gave him a gold ring with the royal seal, a gold chain of office and a fine linen robe to wear. Joseph did his job well and everything he had foretold came true. During the years of plenty, he filled the royal storehouses with tonnes of grain. And when famine struck, the people of Egypt had enough to eat. ▶

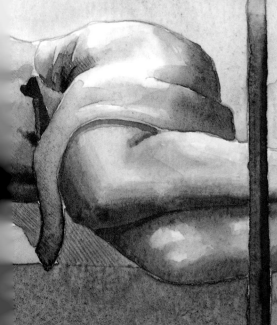

Did you know?

In Ancient Egypt, most people worked as farmers and relied on a good harvest for their food. Each year, the River Nile flooded, spreading thick, rich soil over the plains. This was ideal for growing crops. But if the floodwaters rose too high and ruined the harvest, famine quickly followed. Storing grain for use in times of famine was very important.

Now the famine struck nearby Canaan too. When Jacob heard there was food in Egypt, he sent his sons to buy some. Ten of Joseph's brothers set off, leaving only Benjamin at home with their father. The brothers went to Joseph and bowed down before him. Joseph recognised them at once but they did not know him, so grand had he become. They begged Joseph to give them food. But instead, and to their great dismay, Joseph accused them of being spies and threw them into prison.

"If you want to prove your innocence," he told them, "go home and fetch your youngest brother. But one of you must stay here while the others go."

So Joseph's brothers went to fetch Benjamin, Jacob's youngest son, and returned with him to Egypt. Joseph was overjoyed to see his brother but he could not show his feelings. He gave his brothers a meal, filled their sacks with grain and sent them on their way. He also hid a silver cup in one of their sacks. Just as the brothers were about to set off, Joseph pretended to discover that the cup was missing.

"Woe betide you when I catch the thief," he raged. "Whoever it is will stay behind as my slave."

To the brothers' dismay and disbelief, the silver cup was finally found in the sack on Benjamin's donkey. Surely Benjamin could not have stolen it? Judah begged Joseph to change his mind.

"Make me your slave instead of my brother," he pleaded. "My father has lost one of his favourite sons already. To lose Benjamin would surely kill him."

Then Joseph could not bear it any longer. He told his servants to leave the room. Then, when he was alone with his brothers, he began to weep.

"Don't be afraid," he told them. "I am Joseph, your long-lost brother. You sold me into slavery and God brought me here to save your lives. Now, hurry, go back to Canaan and tell my dear father that I am alive. Bring him back to Egypt with you and your families. From now on, you will live here with me."

So Jacob and his sons went to live with Joseph in Egypt, and it was there that Jacob died.

Did you know?

One of the main messages of Joseph's story is the importance of being genuinely sorry for doing wrong. Joseph puts his brothers in a difficult position to see if they had learned their lesson. After all, they had already abandoned Joseph. Would they now stand by Benjamin or also abandon him? When Joseph sees that they truly have changed, he forgives them for the way they treated them.

The Baby in the Bulrushes

In time, Joseph and his brothers died but their descendants, the Israelites, lived on in Egypt. For a while, their lives were happy. But when a new Pharaoh came to the throne, things changed for the worse. This Pharaoh did not remember Joseph or the good he had done for Egypt. He was afraid the Israelites would take over his land.

Pharaoh treated the Israelites as slaves and set them to work building his royal cities. It was back-breaking work, from dawn to dusk, but the worse things got, the stronger it made the Israelites. One day Pharaoh gave a command:

"Take every new-born baby boy," he told the midwives, "and throw them into the river to drown."

At about this time, an Israelite woman had a baby boy. She hid him in her house. But when he grew too big to hide any more, she made a basket from bulrushes, covered it with tar to make it watertight, and placed the baby in it. Then she hid it among the reeds by the river. The baby's sister waited nearby to see what would happen.

Later that day, Pharaoh's daughter came to bathe in the river. She spotted the basket and sent her maid to fetch it. When she opened the basket, she could not believe her eyes - inside was a baby and he was crying.

The little boy's sister stepped forward.

"Your Highness, I know where to find a good nurse," she said, and went to fetch her mother.

Later, the Pharaoh's daughter adopted the boy and brought him up as her own son in the royal palace. She called him Moses, which means 'drawn out', because she had drawn him out of the water.

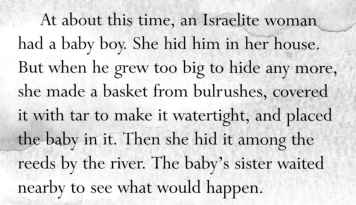

Moses and the Burning Bush

Moses grew up as an Egyptian prince but he never forgot his Israelite family. One day, he saw an Egyptian brutally beating an Israelite slave. When no-one was looking, Moses killed the Egyptian and buried his body in the sand.

When Pharaoh found out, he was furious and ordered Moses to be put to death. But Moses ran away from Egypt, to live in the land of Midian. He married Zipporah, the daughter of a priest called Jethro. While Moses was out in the desert looking after Jethro's flocks, an extraordinary thing happened. Before his eyes, a bush suddenly burst into flames. Although fire licked around the bush, it wasn't burned at all. Then Moses heard God's voice calling to him.

"Moses!" God said. "I have seen my people's troubles in Egypt and have come to save them. You must go to Pharaoh, and ask him to set the Israelites free. Then you will lead them out of Egypt."

Did you know?

Moses became one of the Jews' greatest leaders. But, at first, Moses was reluctant to do what God asked and lead the Israelites out of Egypt. He felt that he could not do such a great thing and made excuses to try to get out of it. But God trusted and believed in Moses and helped him in his task.

The Escape from Egypt

Moses returned to Egypt, as God commanded, and asked Pharaoh to let the Israelites go. But Pharaoh refused and made the Israelites work harder than ever before. Again and again, Moses asked for their freedom but Pharaoh would not listen. So God sent ten terrible plagues to punish the Egyptians. First, the River Nile turned into blood. Then there were plagues of frogs, lice and wild beasts. A horrible disease killed the Egyptians' cattle, and people suffered from painful boils. Storms flattened their fields and locusts ate their crops. Then it was dark as night for three days. But nothing would change Pharaoh's mind. The last plague of all was the most dreadful - every first-born child in Egypt died.

Finally, Pharaoh called Moses to him.

"Take your people and leave," he said. "We do not want any more of your horrible plagues."

So the Israelites gathered their possessions together, and followed Moses out of Egypt into the desert. God sent a cloud to show them the way by day, and a fire to guide them by night. ▶

But when Pharaoh heard that the Israelites had escaped, he changed his mind again and sent his army to fetch them back. The Israelites were trapped. Before them lay a lake called the Sea of Reeds; behind them thundered the Egyptian war-chariots. But God came to their rescue. He sent a wind which drove the waters back so that the Israelites could cross the dry lake bed. Then the waters roared back again, and drowned the Egyptian army.

Three months after leaving Egypt, the Israelites reached Mount Sinai. Their journey had been long and hard, and the people were tired and frightened. Moses told them to pitch camp at the foot of the mountain. Then he climbed to the top to pray to God.

"Go to your people and tell them this. If they obey me, they will be my special people," God told him. "Tell them to

get ready. In three days' time, I will appear again."

On the third day, as the Israelites waited, the sky turned black, and a terrible thunderstorm broke. Lightning flashed around the mountain, which was wrapped in thick curls of smoke. Then, a trumpet sounded its piercing call, louder and louder. God called Moses to the top of the mountain. There he gave Moses ten rules ▶

Did you know?

For the autumn festival of Sukkot, many Jews build a wooden hut called a sukkah in their garden to live in for a while. This reminds them of the make-shift tents and huts in which their ancestors lived as they wandered through the desert. The roofs of the huts are covered in leaves and branches. On a clear night, you must be able to see the stars through the leaves.

19

or laws for the Israelites to follow and obey. God wrote the laws on two tablets of stone and told Moses to teach them to his people.

"Build a golden chest in which to keep the tablets of the law," he said, "and a place where people can worship me."

The Israelites did as God commanded. Then, for forty more years, they wandered through the desert, carrying God's laws with them, until, after many trials and tribulations, God led them safely to the land of Canaan, their Promised Land.

Did you know?

The Books of Teaching, or Torah, which God gave to Moses on Mount Sinai are the most important Jewish scriptures. They contain stories about the creation of the world, the lives of the first Jews and rules to guide Jews through their lives. Copies are handwritten in Hebrew on scrolls for reading in the synagogue.

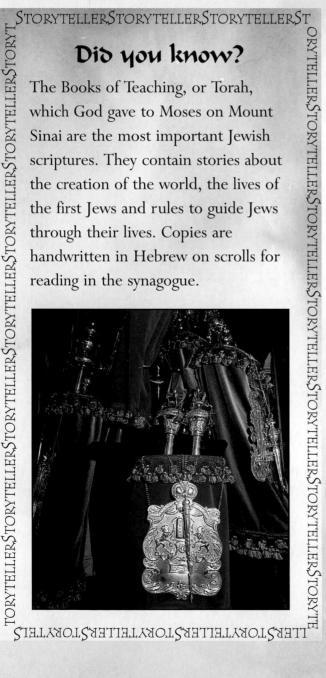

Did you know?

In March or April, Jews remember their ancestors' escape from Egypt with the festival of Pesach. The most important part of the celebrations is a meal called the Seder. Each dish has a special meaning. For example, horse radish is a bitter food. It reminds Jews of how unhappy their ancestors were in Egypt. The egg and lamb bone are offerings to God. The parsley is a sign of hope.

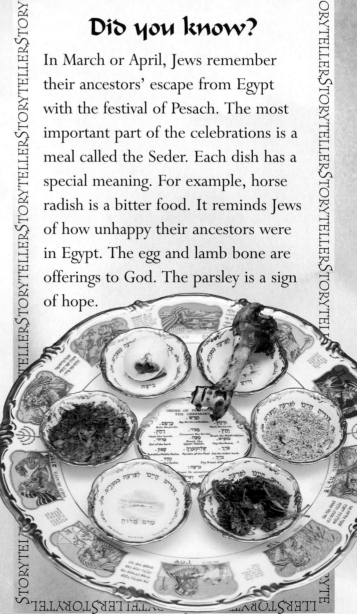

David and Goliath

Long ago, when Saul was king of Israel, a great battle took place between the Israelites and the Philistines. Across the valley, the two sides faced each other, their battle lines drawn. Then a gigantic man stepped forward - the mighty Goliath of Gath. Standing nearly three metres tall, he wore a brass helmet on his head and a massive coat of chain mail. Brandishing a huge iron spear, too heavy for an ordinary man to carry, he threw down his challenge.

"Send your bravest soldier to fight me," he boomed to the Israelites. "If he kills me, the Philistines will become your servants. If I kill him, you will serve us."

The Israelites were terrified. Whatever should they do? Every morning and evening for forty days, Goliath came out and made his challenge.

Some way away, a shepherd boy called David was tending his father's sheep. His three eldest brothers were in Saul's army.

"David," his father said, one day, "Take this bread and cheese to your brothers and bring me news of them."

Did you know?

When Saul died, David became King of Israel and ruled wisely for about forty years. He made his capital in Jerusalem. The Books of Samuel in the Bible tell of his life and works. David is a very important person for the Jews. They believe that he was a great king, scholar and poet who is thought to have written many of the Psalms. According to Jewish tradition, a special leader called the Messiah will come one day. He will be a descendant of King David.

So David set off. But just as he reached his brothers, a hush fell and Goliath once more boomed out his challenge.

"They say that the king has offered a reward," one soldier said. "He'll give great wealth and his daughter's hand in marriage to the person who kills Goliath."

David listened carefully. Then he went to see King Saul.

"I will kill the giant," he said. "God will keep me safe."

So Saul gave David his own helmet and mail coat, and a fine sword. But the armour was too heavy for David. Instead, he picked up his wooden staff and chose five smooth pebbles from a nearby brook. He took the sling he used for scaring off wild beasts as he watched the flocks, and walked over to face Goliath.

The giant laughed when he saw David. "What is this?" he sneered. "A boy come to fight me with sticks and stones?"

Slowly and calmly, David fitted a pebble in his sling and hurled it at the giant. The stone hit Goliath on his forehead, so hard that he fell face down on the ground. Then David ran over and cut off the giant's head.

Seeing their champion dead, the Philistines turned and fled, while the Israelites cheered and shouted. And David went to live in King Saul's palace and married the king's daughter, Michal.

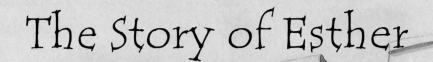

The Story of Esther

There was once a king called Ahasuerus who ruled the great kingdom of Persia which stretched from India to Ethiopia. He lived in a splendid palace, surrounded by luxury. He had a beautiful wife called Esther whom he loved more than anyone else.

Now the king had a prime minister called Haman. He was vain and full of his own importance, ordering everyone he met to bow down before him. And everyone did, all except a Jew called Mordecai, who was also Queen Esther's cousin. Haman was furious with him.

"I order you to bow before me," he ranted and raged.

"I will not," came Mordecai's calm reply.

"Very well," sneered Haman, "but you will suffer for your disobedience."

Then wicked Haman plotted to get his revenge. He would punish all the Jews, not just Mordecai. He went to see his master, King Ahasuerus.

"Your Majesty," he said in a wheedling voice, "It has come to my notice that the Jews in your kingdom do not obey your Majesty's laws. It would surely be better to get rid of these people once and for all?"

▶

Did you know?

The story of Esther is told in the
Bible. At the festival of Purim, in
February or March, many Jews go to
the synagogue to hear the story read
from a scroll. Every time wicked
Haman is mentioned, children try to
make as much noise as possible,
booing, stamping their feet and
shaking rattles, to drown out his name.

"You must do whatever you think is best," said the king.

So Haman gave orders, in the name of the king, that all the Jews in the kingdom should be killed, young and old.

All over the kingdom, there was weeping and mourning, as Haman's evil orders were read out. In despair, Mordecai sent word to his cousin, the queen, to tell her of the Jews' plight. He begged her to go to her husband, the king, and plead for the life of her people. For, being Jewish, her own life was in danger too.

Esther put on her royal robes and went to see the king. She invited the king and Haman to come next day to a banquet, specially prepared for them. She had something important to ask, she said.

Next day, at the banquet, the king said to Esther, "What is your request, dear Esther? Whatever it is, will be granted."

"If it pleases your Majesty," Esther replied. "Spare the lives of my people. And spare my life too, for I am a Jew like them."

Then she told the king the real reason why Haman wanted to kill the Jews, because Mordecai her cousin would not bow to him. The king was furious. He ordered Haman to be hanged, on the very same gallows Haman had built for Mordecai. He also made Mordecai his second-in-command. So this is how brave Queen Esther saved the Jews from the wicked Haman. Every year, her story is still remembered.

Did you know?

Purim is a very joyful time when Jews celebrate the triumph of good over evil. After the synagogue service, people eat special three-cornered cakes, called Hamantaschen (Haman's pockets). There are also fancy-dress parties for children, and Purim plays.

25

Judah Saves the Jews

Many years ago, a Greek king called Antiochus ruled. In every land of his vast empire, he ordered people to give up their gods and worship the Greek gods instead. Only the Jews refused to obey. They worshipped one God and no other. To punish the Jews, Antiochus sent his soldiers to Jerusalem. They ransacked the Temple, the Jews' holiest place, stole its treasures and snuffed out the oil lamp which had always burned there day and night as a symbol of God's presence. A statue of the Greek god, Zeus, was set up in the Temple, and Antiochus ordered that every Jew must sacrifice a pig to Zeus, or face death.

Did you know?

This story is all about people sticking to their own beliefs and values, even when their lives are threatened. The Jews did not want to be forced to stop being themselves or to give up God's commandments. Being different is not easy. But sometimes it is more important to stand up for what you believe.

Not far away, in the small town of Modin, an old priest called Mattathias and his five sons refused to obey the king's command. They killed the soldier who read out the order, then fled to the hills to hide. More and more Jews came to join them, all ready to defy the king. And when Mattathias died, his son, Judah, took command and organised the Jews into an army.

"The king's army may be large and our numbers small," he told the Jews. "But we are fighting for God. He will protect us."

Judah's army fought very bravely, and had many victories against Antiochus's forces, even though they were greatly outnumbered. In time, they drove the enemy out of Jerusalem. Then Judah entered the Temple to repair all the damage that had been done.

"The first thing I must do," Judah said, "is to light the oil lamp's flame again."

But every jar of oil had been broken or spilled. There was none left to light the lamp with. Then Judah spotted a jar hidden in a corner, still with a trickle of oil inside. But there was only enough oil to burn for a day and it would take eight days to fetch any more. Whatever was Judah to do?

Then an amazing thing happened. Judah lit the lamp but it did not go out at the end of the day. Instead it kept on burning for eight whole days, long enough for fresh supplies to arrive.

Did you know?

At the festival of Hanukkah, Jews remember how God kept the Temple lamp burning long ago. They light eight candles, one on the first night, two on the second, and so on until all eight are lit. Hanukkah takes place in December. It is a very happy time for Jews, with special food, presents and parties.

A Shofar in a Coffee Cauldron

In the concentration camp of Bergen Belsen, during World War II, Wolf Fischelberg and his young son, Leo, were walking among the barracks where they and the other Polish Jews lived. They were trying to barter some cigarettes for bread. As they turned the corner, a stone whizzed over their heads from the next-door barracks and landed at their feet. It had been aimed straight at them.

Wolf and Leo looked around anxiously. Then, when they were sure that no one was looking, Wolf bent down and picked up the stone. A piece of paper was wrapped around it. Wolf slipped the note into his pocket and found a safe corner where he could read it. It was from a Dutch Jew called Hayyim Borack.

" I am lucky enough to have a shofar," he wrote, "which you are welcome to use for Rosh Hashanah. I will smuggle it to you in one of the morning coffee cauldrons."

At a time and place planned in the note, a stone was thrown back over the barbed wire fence, accepting Borack's offer.

The shofar was smuggled over without a hitch. But now a new problem arose. For Jewish law said that everyone must be able to hear the sound of the shofar being blown. It was a terrible risk to take. If the Germans caught them, they would pay with their lives.

A great debate took place among the

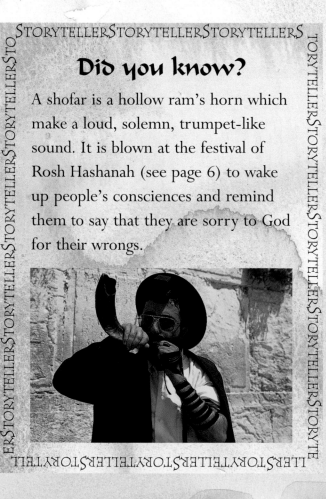

learned rabbis and scholars of the Jews. It was agreed that the shofar should be blown but quietly. Surely God would accept the muffled sound and their prayers.

As Wolf Fischelberg blew the shofar, his little daughter, Miriam, wished that the sound would bring down the barbed-wire fences of Bergen Belsen just as, long ago, it had brought the walls of Jericho tumbling down. But when the service was over, nothing had changed. The barbed-wire fences were still there. But a glimmer of hope stirred in their hearts that, one day, they would be free.

From *Hasidic Tales of the Holocaust*
by Professor Yaffa Eliach

Glossary

Bible The Jewish scriptures. They are also called the Tenakh. They include the Torah.

Canaan The land which we call Israel today.

Commandments Rules or laws which Jews follow in their lives. They tell them how God wants them to behave.

Concentration camp During World War II, millions of Jews were rounded up by the German Nazis and taken to concentration camps. Millions of people were murdered there.

Famine A time when there is very little food to eat.

Holocaust The name given to the murder of millions of Jews, by the German Nazis, in World War II.

Israel A country in the Middle East. Jews believe it is their Promised Land.

Israelites The descendants of Jacob and Joseph. They later became known as the Jews.

Jerusalem The city in Israel where King David made his capital. It is also the capital of modern Israel.

Jew A person who follows the religion of Judaism.

Pharaoh The King of Egypt.

Philistines Enemies of the Israelites.

Promised Land The land of Canaan (now called Israel). Jews believe that God gave them the Promised Land to live in.

Psalms Songs of praise to God. They are often used in Jewish worship.

Rabbis Jewish religious teachers.

Shofar A hollow ram's horn blown at the festival of Rosh Hashanah.

Synagogue A place where Jews go to worship, learn about their religion and meet other Jews.

Temple The Jews' ancient Temple in Jerusalem and the Jews' holiest place. It was built about 3,000 years ago but was later destroyed. Only the Western Wall was left standing. Jews from all the over the world come here to pray.

Torah The most important Jewish holy books. The five books contain stories about the first Jews and rules for Jews to follow.

Index